B

BECOMING ANTIRACIST

A 52 WEEK GUIDED JOURNAL FOR OVERCOMING YOUR RACIST BYPASSING BEHAVIORS

A

L. GLENISE PIKE

BECOMING ANTIRACIST

A 52 WEEK GUIDED JOURNAL FOR OVERCOMING YOUR RACIST BYPASSING BEHAVIORS

L. GLENISE PIKE

A WHERE CHANGE STARTED JOURNAL

About BECOMING ANTIRACIST

BECOMING ANTIRACIST is a 52 week guided journal created for the sole purpose of walking you through the process of becoming antiracist. It is filled with deep-diving, self-reflection journal prompts to guide you on the journey. However, it is also much more than that. BECOMING ANTIRACIST is also a study text that seeks to bring all of the complex topics you've come to know about racism and white supremacy in an overview of the structured process for becoming antiracist.

The Goals of BECOMING ANTIRACIST –

1. To help you make sense of all the antiracism terms and concepts, by putting them into one framework to illustrate how they relate to one another.

2. To provide with a practical blueprint for becoming antiracist.

As you continue to move through BECOMING ANTIRACIST, you'll learn about the following:

The Six Racist Bypassing Behaviors™ that prevent you from becoming antiracist.

The Four Steps to Becoming Antiracist and how they relate to one another.

The four emotional responses to present racism that are the most common **Racial Triggers** for bypassing behavior.

The Racist Tools of Defense you deploy once you've been triggered that perpetuate white supremacy and how to replace those racist tools with **Tools of Accountability**.

The **Journal Prompts** will cover a years worth of self-reflection and hard questions as you journey in antiracism. They are organized in a way to help you discern your most common types of racist bypassing.

This book is about teaching you *how* to become antiracist. It doesn't seek to build the case for antiracism. That should be a given. If you aren't convinced of the importance of antiracism work before attempting to tackle this journal, what I'll have to say throughout this book won't be of use for you. However, if you're ready to dig deep, ask yourself the hard questions, and stare that truth in the face, you're in the right place.

Now that we've gotten that out of the way, I wanted to pause and share a few thoughts with you. This journal is a huge undertaking. It is likely your biggest time commitment yet within the space of antiracism. It's a full year of self reflection and self interrogation work that won't always be fun. You will find yourself wanting to give it a rest and take a break every now and then. That's ok. It's only natural.

I want you to know that even though this journal is laid out weekly and can be completed in a year's time on that schedule, you are still very much free to go at your own pace. The most important thing is that you are doing the work and are honest about the effort you're putting into it.

What To Expect -

The text at the beginning of this journal is meant to provide you with a framework for how you should navigate antiracism responsibly – with this resource and any others you may come across. At the very least, you should commit to reading through those pages in a timely manner. Read them as many times as it takes. Revisit them as you work through the journal. They will be essential to your understanding of what is expected of you as you become antiracist.

In the meantime, I would love for you to keep the following things in mind as you move through this journal as your expectations at the onset are key to being able to see this work through:

1. While I make every effort to talk directly to you throughout this text, you will read the words "white people" repeatedly. If this is a trigger for you that hinders your ability to learn, you'll need to process that now. If you are white, you are included in that phrase. I make no apologies and provide no disclaimers or qualifiers for its use.

2. White supremacy is racism. They are the same thing. I use those words interchangeably. Let's get on the same page about that.

3. Antiracism isn't about your ego. It's not about you being better than other white people. It's not about getting gold stars or ally recognition. It's not about being

able to dawn another label that signals to BIPOC that you're safe without having to prove it.

It's about how your action impact BIPOC. It's about you stopping *your* racist actions, beliefs and practices, not you trying to figure out how to call everyone else's out in the process. Anyone can learn how to identify racism in others. It's an entirely different process to learn how to stop it within oneself.

4. White supremacy is not all that clever and creative. It shows up to enforce its presence in very predictable ways. You may have some catching up to do in regard to developing the eyes for it. However, you *can* learn its patterns of behavior, the tools it uses to reinforce itself, and how they both manifest within you. All it takes is practice and dedication to get there. Don't stop.

5. Be kind to yourself. You are not perfect. You never will be. Striving for perfection in this journey will only lead to the very behaviors you're hoping to eradicate with this work. Extend grace to yourself in this journey. Extend it to others. Progress is a process.

SIX TYPES OF RACIST BYPASSING BEHAVIORS

Racist bypassing is a pattern of behavior that facilitates the avoidance of personal accountability and denial of one's racist behaviors when triggered by the implication of present racism. Those patterns of behavior perpetuate white supremacy by protecting white privilege and ultimately prevent you from becoming antiracist.

The patterns of behaviors discussed in this book are not newly defined phenomena. Many others have written about things like white saviorism, tone-policing, tokenizing, and more. However, antiracism is much more than just a never ending list of woke words and concepts. There is a structure to racism, your responses to it, and the means to which you defend yourself against it. BECOMING ANTIRACIST is my attempt to put all of those terms and concepts into a structured framework to show you how they related to one another. They all serve a purpose. They are a means to an end. That end is the protection of white privilege and upkeeping of white supremacy.

The Six Types of Racist Bypassing Behaviors –

There are six types of racist bypassing behaviors. Meaning, there are six common ways in which you are capable to justifying your way out of dealing with racism by engaging in a pattern of behavior that prevent you from becoming antiracist. The six types are as follows and are in no particular order for this text: politics, spiritual, intersectional, financial, generational, and geographical.

Political Bypassing is the act of relying on any political action, practice, or belief to avoid being held accountable for your racism.

Spiritual/Religious Bypassing is the act of relying on any spiritual or religious action, belief, and practice to avoid being held accountable for your racism.

Intersectional Bypassing is the act of relying on any part of your intersectional identities to avoid being held accountable for your racism.

Financial Bypassing is the act of relying on any financial contribution to Black, Indigenous, or People of Color causes and efforts (often in the form of donations, not purchased goods and services) to avoid being held accountable for you racism.

Generational Bypassing is the act of hiding behind your age to avoid being held accountable for your racism.

Geographical Bypassing is the act of hiding behind where you're from or currently live to avoid being held accountable for your lack of knowledge about racism.

Why You Engage In Racist Bypassing –

Regardless of the type of bypassing behaviors you're prone to, they all manifest themselves in the same patterns of behaviors. Racist bypassing occurs when you witness a call out to racism. That call out can be directed at you or at someone else, the result is basically the same. When the call out is directed at you, you engage in personal racist bypassing. When the call out is directed at someone else, you engage in vicarious racist bypassing.

Vicarious racist bypassing occurs when there is a part of another person's image, lifestyle, personality, or brand that you really identify with getting called out and there is a fear that their behavior get called into question means that yours can as well. So you engage in racist bypassing on their behalf, because if you can wiggle them out of being held accountable in some way, that means you won't have to be accountable, should you ever make the same mistake. Which leads me to why racist bypassing is even a thing. It protects white privilege.

There is a widespread, fundamental misunderstanding of what white privilege is, where it comes from, and the utility it has within this work. That misunderstanding has led many to weaponize their white privilege under the guise of being in allyship with BIPOC.

Have you ever said any derivative of the following statements?:

- "I want to use my white privilege for good."
- "I need to learn more about my white privilege."
- "I've been unpacking my white privilege."
- "How can I use my white privilege to dismantle white supremacy?"

Take a few seconds and really look at those statements for me. Does anything about them stand out to you? It's ok if nothing does. It took me a long time to put my finger on what seemed odd in these words as well. After all, these words have made their rounds in social justice circles for the longest time. Unfortunately, that doesn't change the reality of the fact that these words perpetuate a lie.

These call-to-actions perpetuate the widespread lie that you can "use" white privilege to dismantle white supremacy. You can't.

White privilege is the unearned benefit white and white passing individuals receive for being white in a white supremacist society. It is a product of white supremacy. Therefore, it is a product of racism. It wouldn't exist without white supremacy and white supremacy needs it maintain its signature power imbalance. There is no way the unearned benefit of racism can be used to dismantle white supremacy without perpetuating the very power imbalance created by it. That unearned benefit prioritizes whiteness at its core. It always will.

Take another look at those statements. *My* white privilege. It's a fascinating statement. The use of the word "my" in front of such an automatic and broadly bestowed benefit for simply existing in whiteness within a white supremacist society.

One of the greatest privileges white supremacy gives to whiteness is the benefit of individuality. It is this very benefit that makes it incredibly difficult for white people to understand what it is actually being asked of them when they've been called in to become antiracist. Individuality convinces you that your own version of white privilege looks differently from another person's white privilege. Individuality convinces you that white privilege can be unique to the person and not the blanket benefit that it was created to be. That is wrong.

As long as you think *your* white privilege is different from other people's white privilege, you'll think that your racism makes a different impact than other people's racism. That exercise will always lead you to conclude that the harm you perpetuate though white privilege is of lesser importance than the harm inflicted by others. You'll always think your starting point for the work is different than other people's starting point. This preserves *your* white privilege, while you get to focus on someone else's - except it doesn't work that way.

White privilege is a blanket privilege for being white or white passing. There is nothing you do that makes it anything less than that. What you hold in your back pocket for you through racist bypassing just gets recycled back in the system for everyone else who looks like you.

Why Bypassing Prevents You From Becoming Antiracist –

It perpetuates white supremacy by protecting white privilege and encouraging white saviorism and performative allyship. Both of these are acts that white allies engage in under the guise of helping to dismantle white supremacy that actually only maintain that very system. They are hallmark displays of someone engaging in the community action stage of antiracism without having moved through the deeply self-interrogative stage of antiracism.

To dismantle white supremacy, social power, accesses and opportunity must be decentralized from whiteness and redistributed equally amongst all racist. White saviorism does the opposite of that. White people are still the power brokers within that structure. Instead of redistributing that power, access, and opportunity to BIPOC to do with it as they please, white saviorism serves as a mechanism for white people to acknowledge that they have an unearned privilege, but still hold themselves out as the authority for where those privileges should be enjoyed. The use of one's white privilege to aid BIPOC is simply white supremacy by another name.

How To Stop Your Racist Bypassing Behaviors –

You become antiracist by doing the work and moving through the process where you're learn how to turn your racist tool of defense into tools of accountability. The next section will walk you through what those stages are and what is expected of you as you navigate each one.

THE PROCESS OF BECOMING ANTIRACIST

If racism is a system and white supremacy is racism, then there must be a systematic approach to unlearning the lies taught to you within those structures and dismantling it. There is a process to becoming antiracist. It's not something you just morph into overnight.

You often hear from antiracism educators that "antiracism is lifetime work." If you've spent enough time around Where Change Started, you've likely heard me say the same thing often. It sounds kind of glim and makes the work seem a bit pointless when not placed in the proper context. I get that. I promise it makes a lot more sense when you actually understand what the process of becoming antiracist looks like.

The statement isn't a lie, however. Antiracism is absolutely lifetime work. Meaning, we'll be working to make the world antiracist until the last of our days. However, it does not take a lifetime for you to *become* an antiracist. There really is a clear, obtainable destination at the end to this journey.

What is Antiracism? –

Antiracism is *the act of opposing racism in all its forms.*

It's that simple. I know that you are likely to find plenty of longer definitions for antiracism in a google search, but I like simple. For me, antiracism isn't an academic exercise or a social theory to be overly intellectualized in a classroom setting. It doesn't need to be overly complicated. Antiracism is just the act of opposing racism in all its forms. That includes the forms that exist *within* you.

Racism manifests itself in many forms within our society – person to person, institutional, and systemic. Despite how we speak of them as the boogie men of social justice, institutional and systemic racism didn't come out of nowhere, unfortunately. There were, and still are, individuals behind the creation, implementation, and enforcement of each and every policy, practice, or guideline that perpetuates and upholds white supremacy within our society. Whether we're talking about person to person racism or structural/systemic/institutional racism, it all boils down to individuals making choices. Despite this fact, many believe that the fight to eradicate these different forms of racism depends on the type we're addressing at the time. I couldn't disagree more.

Antiracism is about the individual. It always has been. Individuals are ground zero for racism. We can see the truth of this everywhere today. We need look no further than the election of Barack Obama to see that visibly progressed systems within our country are not a reflection of a lack of racism on the grassroots level. Despite all of the legislative wins and perceived progress being made, those changes are constantly under threat of being rolled back, because change doesn't happen from the top down.

People don't turn their racism off while they're on the job. People don't turn their racism off when they vote. No matter how subtle, if it's there, it's there. It is only through humility and self-interrogation of one's racist behaviors that anyone can even begin to create change outside of themselves. True, sustainable change has to start with the individual or it won't last.

The Process –

The process of becoming antiracist can be broken down into four stages: **awareness, education, self-interrogation, and community action**. Each of these stages are uniquely and equally important in this work. As you read through the overview of these stages below, be thinking about where you stand in this process, where you've been intentional, and be honest about it.

1. THE AWARENESS STAGE – This is the stage you experience your first conscious awakening to the racial issues around you. It is that very first time you pause and register a discrepancy in the narratives you've grown used to hearing.

Awareness is not when you find yourself saying, "I can't believe [insert something about race that most Black, Indigenous, and people of color have lived with every day] is still happening today." It's not just about seeing that a problem exists. Awareness is where you have your light bulb moment and come to realize that a problem not only exists, but that **you play a crucial role in fixing it**.

2. THE EDUCATION STAGE – In the education stage of becoming antiracist, you become a student and begin expanding your understanding of white supremacy. This education includes, but is not limited to, learning definitions of terms and concepts, researching historical accounts and revelations, and staying in the know of present day manifestations of the systemic issues at hand. You do this by intentionally reading books and blogs, signing up for and attending workshops, webinars/seminars, and guest lectures, and completing as much antiracism education curriculum that you can get your hands on.

The education stage often gets mistaken for the "self-work" of antiracism. However, the self-work of antiracism requires much more of you than simply being able to recall stats about how Black women are underserved by medical professionals or how Native Americans have the highest rates of diabetes due to lack of access to fresh food. It needs to you to dig deep and scrutinize your own actions, beliefs, and practices, so that you may begin learning how to stop your *own* racist behaviors.

3. THE SELF-INTERROGATION STAGE – The Self-Interrogation stage of antiracism is where the hard work begins. The first two may be shocking to the conscience, but this is where you begin to put your actions where your intentions are – starting with the one person you have complete control over, which is you. This is the self-work.

This stage isn't about anyone else. It's about you and you alone. It's the place where you start reflecting on the ways your actions, practices, and beliefs may have perpetuated the racism you hope to dismantle. You begin to unpack the ways you reflect white supremacy into the world. You learn ugly truths. You start the process of breaking down the version of you built in white supremacy and rebuild her into a new you that is built in antiracism.

There are three very important steps to moving through the self-interrogation stage of antiracism. FIRST, you must acknowledge your r**acial triggers** that start the process of you attempting to bypass the self-work of antiracism. SECOND, you'll need to identify the **racist tools of defense** you deploy to accomplish that bypassing. LAST, you will need to replace those tools of defense with **tools of accountability** that limit your ability to weaponize white supremacy against Black, Indigenous, and People of Color.

4. THE COMMUNITY ACTION STAGE – The Community Action Stage is where your words, actions, and impact are meant to help facilitate change within the world you navigate. It's what I like to call the "do something" stage, because when white people ask me how they can become antiracist, it's usually this part of the work they are asking me about.

> This stage of antiracism gets a lot of people in trouble. THIS is where racist bypassing turns into harm. Engaging in stage four of antiracism without having done stage three is how so many people end up engaging in white saviorism and many of the other racist behaviors that hurt BIPOC.

The first two stages of becoming antiracist are the most common lived in stages of the process. That part of this work never truly stops, but it's not enough to help you stop committing and perpetuating racist acts. For that reason, the remainder of the text in this journal will primarily focus on the Self-Interrogation stage of becoming antiracist.

I'll walk you through your racial triggers, the tools of defense that are commonly deployed when bypassing and how to turn them into tools of accountability. I will then share some accountability tips for getting out of the way and navigating community action in a way that honors Black, Indigenous, and people of color the way they deserved to be honored in this work.

Understanding Your Emotional Triggers To Racism

White and white passing people harm BIPOC by weaponizing their white privilege out of a response to hurt. A hurt they have never had to deal with prior to being consciously aware of racism and their ability to perpetuate it. After all, white supremacy prioritizes whiteness, so there would be no need for you to develop the layer of thick skin to understand that the progress you claim to champion in antiracism will require that you give up the right to feel comfortable all of the time.

There are four main racial triggers that stop you from becoming antiracist through the process of racist bypassing: **anger**, **guilt**, **fear**, and **shame**. While they manifest differently in every person, these emotions ultimately lead you to arm yourself with racist tools of defense to protect your conscience from whatever truths you don't want to admit. Understanding the emotional responses you experience when you're exposed to racism is a key first step in the self-interrogation stage of becoming antiracist.

It doesn't really matter which emotion you're feeling, honestly. All four of these emotional triggers are born out of places of misplaced expectations for yourself and others. It would be impossible for me to diagnose exactly why you feel what you feel when being called out for racism. All that I can say for sure is that they contradict the misplaced expectations you have for yourself and others, leading you to act out in pain and ultimately weaponizing white privilege against BIPOC. The following are a few examples of how I've seen these emotions manifest in individuals attempting engage in racist bypassing.

Anger:
Anger that you've been accused harming BIPOC despite your intentions.
Anger that your good deeds don't outweigh your bad ones.
Anger that you're being likened to people you think you're better than.
Anger that no matter what you do, BIPOC approach you with suspicion, instead of treating you like the safe person you want to be for them.

Guilt:
Guilt for hurting someone.
Guilt for slacking off in your education and missing the opportunity to prevent a foreseeable display of racism.
Guilt for not speaking up when you thought you should.
Guilt for not being antiracist yet.

Fear:
Fear of acknowledging the hurt you've caused BIPOC.
Fear that you're not as good a person you once thought you were.
Fear that you don't have what it takes to become antiracist.
Fear of sitting too long in the discomfort.

Shame:
Shame for not knowing better.
Shame for knowing better, but not caring enough to pay attention.
Shame for feeling battle fatigue in the fight when BIPOC have to deal with racism every day.
Shame for sheltering yourself from the painful stories and retreating back into the safety of white privilege.

The list can literally go on. If you've felt anything like this, nine times out of ten, you've armed yourself with a racist tool of defense to get out of feeling that way for too long.

Unpacking Your Emotional Responses to Racism –

I can't tell you exactly why you feel these emotions when you do, but I can give you a list of questions that you can ask yourself when that discomfort starts to creep up and you feel yourself attempting to reach for a tool of defense.

1. What emotions am I feeling?
2. What did I previously believe about myself that this new information is contradicting?
3. What do I think this information says about me now?
4. How can I use what I've just learned about myself to make me better going forward?

I'm certain there are many more questions you can ask when you feel yourself reacting out of hurt for being called out. However, these four are absolutely necessary.

Keep them close, because there is no place in this journey where you will be able to avoid being triggered by racism forever. The goal of this work is simply to teach you how to arm yourself with tools of accountability, rather than tools of defense when that time comes.

Identify Your Racist Tools of Defense

Step two of the self-interrogation stage of becoming antiracist requires you to identify the racist tools you arm yourself with when you feel triggered by a call out. Every single item on this list (and the many didn't make it) is a weapon that makes you incredibly dangerous to BIPOC when navigating spaces of antiracism without having done the work to disarm yourself of them. Without the intentional work of understanding your emotional responses to racial triggers, deploying these tools will continue to be your automatic reaction when that happens.

A racist tool of defense is an action that does at least one of the following:

1. Centers your comfort and perspective
2. Invalidates BIPOC lived experiences
3. Elevate palatable BIPOC voices while silencing others
4. Makes you the victim

Tokenism – if you've ever mentioned or thought of your relationships with BIPOC as a reason for why you couldn't be racist or why your actions couldn't be too harmful, then you're tokenizing. When you tokenize your BIPOC friends, family, and colleagues, you are attempting to protect yourself from being held accountable for your racism by literally placing black and brown bodies in front of you as a human shield. Your response to being called out for harming BIPOC is to put more in harm's way on your behalf. This action centers your white comfort to the detriment of BIPOC.

Intellectualizing – attempting to rationalize your way out of racism applying to you in any given situation is intellectualizing. It allows you to disassociate from the conversation emotionally, but it also invalidates BIPOC lived experiences.

Consensus Building – when you've been called out for your racism by a BIPOC, if you find yourself searching for voices to tell you that you aren't racist or that your actions weren't that bad, you're consensus building. This tool of defense allows you to avoid accountability by invalidating the voice and experience of the BIPOC who came to you in the first place. It doesn't matter at all if every other BIPOC you know disagrees with that person, their feelings are still valid.

White supremacy would have you think that white people were the only ones who deserved the benefit of individuality, but that is a lie (one you'll be unlearning in the process of becoming antiracist). Not all BIPOC would call out the same behaviors. Every BIPOC has a different threshold for the emotional labor they're willing to do in this work. Finding BIPOC voices that validate you, but not the person who called you out is silencing accountability.

Tone-Policing – cherry-picking which voices you are willing to listen to based on how nice they are to you is tone-policing. This can be done directly following a call-out by pointing out tone as a retort to claims of racism or by the way you curate voices to learn from on your journey to become antiracist. That is not to say that teaching style isn't something you shouldn't consider when investing in your antiracism education. It is. The goal is for you to learn. However, not every piece of triggering content or interaction with BIPOC that you encounter will be from that perspective. You can't expect that every encounter you have with racism will be one that comes from a place of educational patience.

Focusing on how someone said something, rather than what they actually said, is just a way for you to avoid being held accountable for your racism by making yourself the victim of their harsh tone. Tone-policing allows you to shield yourself from accountability because it gives you the ability to maintain control over your environment and comfort, while purporting to want to learn. You get to move the goal post for what is or isn't an acceptable tone any time it benefits you. This centers you and your comfort, while silencing BIPOC you never intended to listen to in the first place.

There are many other tools you can arm yourself with when being triggered by racism. These are just a few examples to illustrate the elements of what makes an action a racist tool of defense. The key takeaway for you here is that if your emotional response to being called out for racism leads you to engage in any actions that does one of those four things, you've armed yourself with a racist tool of defense. If that is the case, you'll need to understand why you've done that. There are few questions you can ask yourself to discern why that is the case:

1. What part of me or my identity am I feeling compelled to protect?
2. What do I think I'll lose other than comfort in the moment, if I were to sit with this?
3. How did this reaction invalidate the lived experience of BIPOC in this conversation or in general?

Stopping Your Racism: Developing Your Tools of Accountability

Once you've identified the racist tools of defense you deploy after being triggered, you should begin the process of turning them into tools of accountability. Tools of defense feed the underlying emotions the lead you to racial bypassing and places the burden on BIPOC to keep you from experiencing those emotions and thus stopping you from behaving in racist ways. Tools of accountability leave the work where it belongs – with you.

It bears repeating that becoming antiracist doesn't mean that you will stop being racially triggered by call outs and call ins. You will. Being antiracist simply means that instead of behaving in racist ways to avoid accountability, you lean into that accountability instead. It means that you no longer automatically reach for those tools of defense to weaponize your white privilege. This will take practice. Lots of practice. You will not be perfect in this process. However, it is entirely possible for you to replace your racist habits with ones that hold you accountable.

Here are a couple of ways you can do that. This list is far from exhaustive, because tools of accountability can look very different for everyone. Only you'll know what you need to do in order to stop arming yourself with racist tools. These are just a few suggestions for you as you start the process of finding your own.

1. Use Pronouns That Are Inclusive of You

The words you use matter. They guide you and represent your intentions, even when you don't realize it. When talking about white supremacy, it's important that you use pronouns that are inclusive of you. When talking about white people, say "us" and "we," instead of "they" or "them." Your words should be a clear indication that you aren't seeking to differentiate yourself or your racist behaviors from that of others.

2. Be Clear About Your Desired Impact.

Antiracism is about the impact of your actions on Black, Indigenous, and People of Color, not you intention. Ask yourself what impact you're hoping to make in this work – on yourself and others and in any given situation where you're encountering emotional triggers call outs.

Create a mission statement that embodies what that is and lead with it. Keep it in a place that is readily assessible to you. Refer back to it as many times are you need to. This will be a great way to remind yourself of your "why" when things on this journey get frustrating.

3. **Listen.**

This one should be a given, but I'll say it anyway. Listen more than you talk. Whether you've been triggered by a call out directed at you or one directed at someone you identify with, you'll have the tendency to attempt to talk yourself out of it. Be quiet for a while and let that urge pass before you speak.

4. **Adopt a Growth Mindset**

You cannot do this work if you are not humble about it. Perfectionism is the greatest hindrance to progress. You're going to fail at this in the beginning. Even if you've failed a lot up to this point, it doesn't mean that you can't overcome what has caused you to do that. Don't be afraid to try again when you get things wrong. Practice is the only way you'll be better at this.

5. **Always Examine Your Motives & Question Yourself**

Unlearning the lies white supremacy has taught you will take time. Everything you think is normal and everything you've been taught to prioritize has been steeped in white supremacy. Question all of it.

Becoming Antiracist is a process. There is no magic bullet. It's going to take time and practice for you to overcome your racist bypassing behaviors. A great place to start that practice is by being consistent in your self-interrogation. Some days, you'll learn a lot about yourself. Other, you'll learn less. The important part is that you are intention and honest about what those truths are.

THE JOURNAL

WEEK

1

WRITE DOWN YOUR DEFINITION OF WHITENESS. WHAT DOES WHITE IDENTITY MEAN TO YOU? HOW DO YOU SEE IT INTERACT WITH YOUR OTHER IDENTITIES? HOW HAS IT AFFECTED THE WAY YOU RELATE TO THE WORLD.

WEEK

02

MAKE A LIST OF ALL THE NON-RACE RELATED POLITICAL TOPICS YOU'VE SUBCONSCIOUSLY ASSOCIATED WITH THE POSSIBILITY OF SOMEONE'S RACISM OR ALLYSHIP. WRITE ABOUT THE POLITICS YOU IDENTIFY WITH. WHAT ARE THE ISSUES YOU'RE MOST PASSIONATE ABOUT? DO YOU BELONG TO A PARTICULAR POLITICAL PARTY? WHAT DOES IT SAY ABOUT YOU? WHAT ABOUT YOUR UNDERSTANDING OF HOW RACE AND WHITE SUPREMACY AFFECT THOSE TOPICS.

WEEK 03

WRITE ABOUT THE WAYS YOUR EVERYDAY ACTIONS FALL SHORT OF THE PERSONAL ANTIRACIST BRAND YOU SHARE WITH THE WORLD. DO YOU READ EVERYTHING YOU SAY YOU READ? DO YOU SUPPORT BUSINESS THAT PROFIT OFF BLACK, INDIGENOUS, AND PEOPLE OF COLOR CULTURE AND PAIN? ARE YOU INTENTIONAL AND CONSISTENT IN MAINTAINING YOUR EDUCATION?

WEEK

04

REFLECTION WEEK:

WHAT THEMES HAVE STOOD OUT TO YOU OVER THESE PAST FEW WEEKS? WHAT ARE THREE (3) THINGS YOU CAN DO TO INSPIRE BEHAVIORAL SHIFTS IN THESE AREAS OF YOUR ANTIRACISM JOURNEY?

WEEK
05

WRITE ABOUT WHO YOU WERE WHEN YOU STARTED ON YOUR JOURNEY TO BECOMING ANTIRACIST. WHAT WAS THE PRECIPITATING EVENT OR CIRCUMSTANCE THAT FINALLY RESONATED WITH YOU AND INSPIRED YOU TO BECOME AN ACTIVE PARTICIPANT IN DISMANTLING WHITE SUPREMACY? WHO ARE YOU NOW? WHO DO YOU HOPE TO BECOME? WHAT ARE YOU DOING TO BECOME THAT VERSION OF YOU?

WEEK
06

WHAT DO YOU FEAR MOST WHEN IT COMES TO THE WORK OF ANTIRACISM? WHAT GIVES YOU PAUSE? WHAT MAKES YOU QUESTION YOURSELF MOST?

WRITE AN AFFIRMATION OF ENCOURAGEMENT AT THE END OF THIS ENTRY THAT SPEAKS TO THAT FEAR. PUT IT SOMEWHERE YOU'LL SEE IT OFTEN.

WEEK

07

WRITE ABOUT WHY IT IS SO IMPORTANT FOR YOU TO MAKE SURE BLACK, INDIGENOUS, AND PEOPLE OF COLOR KNOW THAT YOU AREN'T ONE OF "THOSE" RACIST WHITE PEOPLE. DO YOU THINK THERE IS A WAY FOR YOU TO GET THAT MESSAGE ACROSS WITHOUT RANKING RACISM AND DEEMING YOURS LESS IMPACTFUL? HOW DOES THAT MAKE ROOM FOR THE LIVED REALITY OF BIPOC EXPERIENCES? HOW WOULD YOUR ANTIRACISM WORK BE IMPACTED, IF BIPOC DIDN'T INITIALLY BELIEVE YOU?

WEEK

08

REFLECTION WEEK:

WHAT THEMES HAVE STOOD OUT TO YOU OVER THESE PAST FEW WEEKS? WHAT ARE THREE (3) THINGS YOU CAN DO TO INSPIRE BEHAVIORAL SHIFTS IN THESE AREAS OF YOUR ANTIRACISM JOURNEY?

WEEK
09

WRITE ABOUT THE THINGS YOU HAVE IN COMMON WITH WHITE PEOPLE ON THE OPPOSITE POLITICAL SPECTRUM FROM YOU? IN WHAT WAY DO YOU THINK YOU'RE BETTER? IN WHAT WAYS DO YOU THINK THEY ARE BETTER? IN WHAT WAYS DO BOTH OF YOU UPHOLD WHITE SUPREMACY?

WEEK

10

WRITE ABOUT THE LAST BIPOC WHOSE WORK YOU READ, LISTENED TO, OR WATCHED AS PART OF YOUR ANTIRACISM EDUCATION. WHY DID YOU PICK THAT PERSON? WHAT ABOUT THEM MADE YOU WANT TO LEARN FROM THEM AND NOT SOMEONE ELSE?

WEEK

11

WRITE ABOUT THE WAYS IN WHICH YOU COULD BE MORE CONSISTENT WITH YOUR ANTIRACISM EFFORTS. BE HONEST ABOUT THE WORK YOU'VE PUT IN. DON'T SHY AWAY FROM YOUR FAILURES. WHAT HAVE YOU COMMITTED TO THAT YOU'VE ACTUALLY FOLLOWED THROUGH ON? WHAT DID YOU LEARN? WHAT NEXT STEPS CAN YOU TAKE TO EXPOUND UPON THOSE LESSONS? HOW COULD YOU BECOME MORE INTENTIONAL IN THE FUTURE TO COMPLETE MORE?

WEEK

12

REFLECTION WEEK:

WHAT THEMES HAVE STOOD OUT TO YOU OVER THESE PAST FEW WEEKS? WHAT ARE THREE (3) THINGS YOU CAN DO TO INSPIRE BEHAVIORAL SHIFTS IN THESE AREAS OF YOUR ANTIRACISM JOURNEY?

WEEK
13

WRITE ABOUT THE TIME YOU MESSED UP IN THE ANTIRACISM SPACE. WRITE OUT IN DETAIL WHAT HAPPENED. HAVE YOU COME TO FULLY APPRECIATE THE HARM YOU CAUSED? HOW DID YOU GET TO THAT PLACE OF UNDERSTANDING? HOW DO YOU FEEL NOW? WHAT LESSONS DID YOU LEARN FROM THE INCIDENT – IN HOW NOT TO DO IT AGAIN AND IN HOW YOU'LL RESPOND IN THE FUTURE?

WEEK 14

WRITE ABOUT HOW YOU HANDLED IT WHEN A BLACK, INDIGENOUS, OR PERSON OF COLOR CALLED YOU OUT WHEN YOU THOUGHT YOU WERE BEING AN ALLY. HOW DID YOU WEAPONIZED YOUR PRIVILEGE AGAINST THEM TO AVOID COMING TO TERMS WITH YOUR COMPLICITY OF WHITE SUPREMACY? WHAT TOOLS OF DEFENSE DID YOU USE?

WEEK 15

In what ways have you continued to feel shame as you journey to become antiracist? What expectations did you have for yourself? How have those helped or hurt your efforts? What words of encouragement could you give yourself to set that emotion aside?

WEEK 16

REFLECTION WEEK:

WHAT THEMES HAVE STOOD OUT TO YOU OVER THESE PAST FEW WEEKS? WHAT ARE THREE (3) THINGS YOU CAN DO TO INSPIRE BEHAVIORAL SHIFTS IN THESE AREAS OF YOUR ANTIRACISM JOURNEY?

WEEK
17

WRITE ABOUT YOUR EXPECTATIONS FOR YOURSELF ON THIS JOURNEY OF BECOMING ANTIRACIST. WHAT DO YOU PLAN TO DO WITH YOU KNEW AWARENESS? HOW DO YOU INTEND TO USE IT TO MAKE YOU BETTER? REMEMBER: KEEP THE FOCUS ON YOU.

WEEK

18

Write about the last time you called someone else out for their racism. List the things you said to them in as much detail as possible. Now go down that list and write the last time you self-reflected in that area. What did you learn about yourself?

WEEK
19

WRITE ABOUT A TIME WHEN YOU TRIED TO HELP (EITHER BY SAYING OR DOING SOMETHING) A BLACK, INDIGENOUS, OR PERSON OF COLOR AND THEY DID NOT RECEIVE IT THE WAY THOUGHT THEY WOULD. LIST WHAT YOUR EXPECTATIONS WERE. WHAT DO YOU THINK THEIR REACTION SAID ABOUT YOU? IN WHAT WAYS DID YOUR DESIRE TO HELP REFLECT WHITE SAVIORISM?

WEEK

20

REFLECTION WEEK:

WHAT THEMES HAVE STOOD OUT TO YOU OVER THESE PAST FEW WEEKS? WHAT ARE THREE (3) THINGS YOU CAN DO TO INSPIRE BEHAVIORAL SHIFTS IN THESE AREAS OF YOUR ANTIRACISM JOURNEY?

WEEK

21

WRITE ABOUT ALL THE WAYS IN WHICH WHITENESS HAS BEEN THE DEFAULT IN YOUR LIFE. EXAMINE EVERYTHING FROM THE SHOWS YOU WATCH TO THE MAKERS YOU BUY FROM. LIST THE WAYS YOU CAN INTENTIONALLY COUNTER THOSE NARRATIVES WITHIN YOUR OWN LIFE. NOW THINK ABOUT THE WAYS YOU CAN COUNTER THOSE NARRATIVES IN YOUR WORKPLACE.

WEEK

22

WRITE ABOUT THE WAYS YOU HAVE LET YOUR OWN DEFINITION OF WHAT IT MEANS TO BE BLACK, INDIGENOUS, ASIAN, LATINX, ETC. INFORM YOUR MOVEMENTS IN ANTIRACISM. THINK ABOUT THE VOICES OF INDIVIDUALS WITHIN THOSE GROUPS THAT YOU LISTEN TO. WHAT ARE THEIR EDUCATIONAL BACKGROUNDS? WHAT TONES DO THEY USE? HOW DO THOSE THINGS IMPACT THE WAY YOU ABSORB THEIR WORDS?

WEEK

23

WRITE ABOUT WHAT INTERSECTIONALITY MEANS TO YOU. IN WHAT WAYS HAVE YOU RESTED BEHIND PARTS OF YOUR IDENTITY TO AVOID HOLDING YOURSELF ACCOUNTABLE FOR YOUR RACISM? IN WHAT WAYS HAVE YOU WEAPONIZED WHITENESS ACROSS GENDER LINES OR RELIGIOUS AFFILIATIONS TO SILENCE BLACK, INDIGENOUS, AND PEOPLE OF COLOR WHO SHARE THOSE OTHER IDENTITIES WITH WITH YOU?

WEEK

24

REFLECTION WEEK:

WHAT THEMES HAVE STOOD OUT TO YOU OVER THESE PAST FEW WEEKS? WHAT ARE THREE (3) THINGS YOU CAN DO TO INSPIRE BEHAVIORAL SHIFTS IN THESE AREAS OF YOUR ANTIRACISM JOURNEY?

WEEK 25

WRITE ABOUT THE LAST POST ABOUT RACISM THAT CAUGHT YOUR ATTENTION. WHAT IT POSITIVE AND CELEBRATING BLACK, INDIGENOUS, AND PEOPLE OF COLOR? OR WAS IT NEGATIVE AND HIGHLIGHTING TRAGEDY, LOSS, AND PAIN? ON AVERAGE, HOW SIMILAR ARE THE MAJORITY OF THE OTHER POSTS THAT CATCH YOUR ATTENTION? WHY DO YOU THINK YOU RESPOND TO THOSE POSTS MORE? HOW HAVE YOU ATTEMPTED TO PUSH YOURSELF OUT OF THAT COMFORT ZONE WITH THE CONTENT YOU CONSUME?

WEEK
26

WRITE ABOUT WHAT IT FEELS LIKE WHEN SOMEONE SAYS THE WORDS "WHITE PEOPLE." IS YOUR RESPONSE DIFFERENT DEPENDING ON WHO SAYS IT? FRIENDS OR FAMILY? WHITE PEOPLE OR BLACK, INDIGENOUS, AND PEOPLE OF COLOR? IF THERE IS A DIFFERENCE? WHY DO YOU THINK THAT IS?

WEEK

27

WRITE ABOUT ANY EXPECTATIONS OF RECOGNITION YOU HAVE AS AN ANTIRACIST IN TRAINING. HOW IMPORTANT IS IT FOR WHITE PEOPLE TO KNOW OF YOUR NEW KNOWLEDGE AND GOOD DEEDS IN THIS SPACE? WHY IS THAT THE CASE? HOW WOULD YOUR ANTIRACISM WORK BE IMPACTED IF NO WHITE PERSON EVER RECOGNIZED IT?

WEEK
28

REFLECTION WEEK:

WHAT THEMES HAVE STOOD OUT TO YOU OVER THESE PAST FEW WEEKS? WHAT ARE THREE (3) THINGS YOU CAN DO TO INSPIRE BEHAVIORAL SHIFTS IN THESE AREAS OF YOUR ANTIRACISM JOURNEY?

WEEK

29

WHAT WAS THE LAST THING YOU SHARED ON SOCIAL MEDIA REGARDING RACE AND WHITE SUPREMACY? WHY DID YOU SHARE IT? WHAT HAD YOU HOPED WOULD HAPPEN? DID IT? GO BACK AND REREAD IT. IS THERE ANYTHING YOU CAN SAY DIFFERENTLY TO DEEPEN YOURS OR OTHER'S UNDERSTANDING OF THE POINT YOU WERE TRYING TO MAKE?

WEEK
30

WRITE ABOUT HOW YOU FEEL WHEN YOUR VOICE IS NOT NEEDED OR WELCOMED IN A CONVERSATION ABOUT RACE. HOW DID IT MAKE YOU FEEL? HOW DID IT AFFECT YOUR DESIRE TO CONTINUE WORKING TOWARD BECOMING ANTIRACIST?

WEEK

31

WRITE ABOUT THE LAST TIME YOU CONTRIBUTED TO A CAUSE CREATED BY OR FOR THE BENEFIT OF BLACK, INDIGENOUS, AND PEOPLE OF COLOR. WHAT EMOTION COMPELLED YOU TO DONATE? WHAT DID THAT DONATION SAY ABOUT YOU? HOW MUCH DID YOU ENGAGE WITH THE TOPIC THAT CALLED FOR THE DONATION?

WEEK

32

REFLECTION WEEK:

WHAT THEMES HAVE STOOD OUT TO YOU OVER THESE PAST FEW WEEKS? WHAT ARE THREE (3) THINGS YOU CAN DO TO INSPIRE BEHAVIORAL SHIFTS IN THESE AREAS OF YOUR ANTIRACISM JOURNEY?

WEEK 33

Write about a time you grew fatigued by the constant stream of racial violence that you've encountered. What did you do to get relief? Looking back, do you think those actions honored the lived experiences of Black, Indigenous, and People of Color? If not, what would you do differently?

WEEK

34

WHAT IS ONE PIECE OF ADVICE YOU WOULD LIKE TO TELL TEENAGE YOU ABOUT SYSTEMIC RACISM AND WHITE SUPREMACY? WHAT WOULD YOU SAY TO THAT PERSON TO ENCOURAGE AND EMPOWER THEM TO BE THE CHANGE AGENT YOU DESIRE TO BE TODAY? WHY WOULD YOUNGER YOU NEED TO HEAR THIS?

WEEK

35

WRITE ABOUT THE WAYS IN WHICH YOU COULD BE MORE CONSISTENT WITH YOUR ANTIRACISM EFFORTS. BE HONEST ABOUT THE WORK YOU'VE PUT IN. DON'T SHY AWAY FROM YOUR FAILURES. WHAT HAVE YOU COMMITTED TO THAT YOU'VE ACTUALLY FOLLOWED THROUGH ON? WHAT DID YOU LEARN? WHAT NEXT STEPS CAN YOU TAKE TO EXPOUND UPON THOSE LESSONS? HOW YOU COULD BECOME MORE INTENTIONAL IN THE FUTURE TO COMPLETE THEM?

WEEK

36

REFLECTION WEEK:

WHAT THEMES HAVE STOOD OUT TO YOU OVER THESE PAST FEW WEEKS? WHAT ARE THREE (3) THINGS YOU CAN DO TO INSPIRE BEHAVIORAL SHIFTS IN THESE AREAS OF YOUR ANTIRACISM JOURNEY?

WEEK
37

WRITE ABOUT THE EMOTIONAL LABOR FROM BLACK, INDIGENOUS, AND PEOPLE OF COLOR THAT YOU'VE BENEFITTED FROM ON YOUR JOURNEY TO BECOMING ANTIRACIST. CONSIDER WHAT THAT LABOR COSTS THEM. WHAT HAS IT COST YOU – DIRECTLY OR INDIRECTLY? WHAT HAVE YOU HAD TO GIVE UP? SPACE? POWER? MONEY? REPUTATION? COMFORT? PLATFORM? SOCIAL STATUS OR PROFESSIONAL POSITIONING? FRIENDS? FAMILY? NOTHING AT ALL?

WEEK
38

WRITE ABOUT A TIME WHEN WHAT YOU LEARNED ABOUT ANTIRACISM FROM ONE BLACK, INDIGENOUS, OR PERSON OF COLOR THAT CONTRADICTED THE LIVED EXPERIENCE ANOTHER BLACK, INDIGENOUS, OR PERSON OF COLOR WAS SHARING WITH YOU IN THE MOMENT? WHAT WAS THE CONVERSATION ABOUT? WHICH PERSPECTIVE DID YOU GIVE MORE WEIGHT TO. WHY?

WEEK 39

WRITE ABOUT A TIME SOMEONE YOU ADMIRED WAS ACCUSED OF BEING RACIALLY INSENSITIVE OR RACIST? HOW DID THAT MAKE YOU FEEL? DID YOU FEEL COMPELLED TO RUN TO THEIR AID? (EVEN IF IT WAS JUST SOCIAL MEDIA CONVERSATIONS) WHY? WHAT PARTS OF THEIR CALL OUT DID YOU FEEL PERSONALLY?

WEEK 40

REFLECTION WEEK:

WHAT THEMES HAVE STOOD OUT TO YOU OVER THESE PAST FEW WEEKS? WHAT ARE THREE (3) THINGS YOU CAN DO TO INSPIRE BEHAVIORAL SHIFTS IN THESE AREAS OF YOUR ANTIRACISM JOURNEY?

WEEK 41

WRITE ABOUT THE FIRST TIME YOU REALIZED YOU WERE WHITE. THE TIME YOU *REALLY* REALIZED IT. DESCRIBE THE CIRCUMSTANCES AND HOW THAT NEW WAY OF SEEING THE WORLD MADE YOU FEEL. WHAT DID IT MAKE YOU FEEL ABOUT YOURSELF? WHAT DID IT MAKE YOU FEEL ABOUT THE OTHER WHITE PEOPLE AROUND YOU?

WEEK
42

WRITE ABOUT THE FIRST TIME YOU WERE ACCUSED OF BEING RACIST. HOW DID IT FEEL? HOW DID YOU RESPOND? WHAT TOOLS OF ACCOUNTABILITY WOULD YOU DEPLOY IF YOU COULD DO IT ALL OVER AGAIN?

WEEK

43

IF YOU COULD WRITE A LETTER TO THE VERSION OF YOURSELF BEFORE STARTING THIS WORK, WHAT WOULD YOU SAY?

WEEK

44

REFLECTION WEEK:

WHAT THEMES HAVE STOOD OUT TO YOU OVER THESE PAST FEW WEEKS? WHAT ARE THREE (3) THINGS YOU CAN DO TO INSPIRE BEHAVIORAL SHIFTS IN THESE AREAS OF YOUR ANTIRACISM JOURNEY?

WEEK 45

WRITE ABOUT THE LAST TIME YOU HAD AN EMOTIONALLY CHARGED CONVERSATION ABOUT RACE? WAS THERE A PERSONAL RELATIONSHIP WITH THIS PERSON? WHAT DID THE CONVERSATION COST YOU? WHAT WAS LOST? WAS IT RESOLVED? DID YOU LEARN ANYTHING NEW ABOUT YOURSELF? DID YOU LEARN ANYTHING NEW ABOUT THE PERSON YOU WERE TALKING TO? HOW HAS THAT NEW KNOWLEDGE IMPACTED HOW YOU'VE INTERACTED WITH YOURSELF AND OTHERS AS AN ANTIRACIST?

WEEK

46

WRITE ABOUT THE WAYS YOU'VE FINANCIALLY CONTRIBUTED TO ANTIRACISM EFFORTS ASIDE FROM DONATIONS? IN WHAT WAYS CAN YOU DO BETTER IN THIS AREA? MOVE BEYOND GENERAL CALLS TO SUPPORT BIPOC BUSINESSES AND EDUCATORS AND GET SPECIFIC TO YOUR NEEDS AND PLANS FOR PERSONAL GROWTH.

WEEK

47

WRITE ABOUT THE AREA OF ANTIRACISM WORK THAT HAS HUMBLED YOU THE MOST. HOW HAS THAT IMPACTED THE WAY YOU INTERACT WITH OTHERS WHO ARE ALSO WORKING TO BECOME ANTIRACIST? HOW HAS THAT IMPACTED THE WAY YOU INTERACT WITH BIPOC?

WEEK 48

WHAT AREA OF GROWTH HAVE YOU EXPERIENCE OVER THIS LAST YEAR THAT YOU ARE MOST PROUD OF? WHAT SUSTAINED THAT PROCESS FOR YOU? HOW CAN YOU APPLY THOSE LESSONS TO OTHER AREAS OF YOUR ANTIRACISM WORK?

WEEK
49

WRITE A MISSION STATEMENT TO GUIDE YOU AS YOUR CONTINUE THIS WORK. WHO DO YOU WANT TO BE? WHAT IMPACT DO YOU WANT TO MAKE? HOW CAN YOU DO THIS IS IN A WAY THAT HONORS BLACK, INDIGENOUS, AND PEOPLE OF COLOR?

WEEK
50

WHAT ARE YOUR ANTIRACISM GOALS NOW THAT YOU'RE ALMOST DONE WITH THIS JOURNAL? WRITE THEM DOWN. WHAT DO YOU NEED TO DO TO ACCOMPLISH THEM?

WEEK
51

CREATE AN ACCOUNTABILITY STRATEGY BASED ON THE MOST COMMON WAYS YOU SOUGHT TO BYPASS PERSONAL ACCOUNTABILITY IN THE PAST.

BE AS SPECIFIC AS POSSIBLE.

WEEK

52

REFLECTION WEEK:

WHAT THEMES HAVE STOOD OUT TO YOU OVER THE COURSE OF THIS LAST YEAR? WHAT ARE THREE (3) THINGS YOU CAN DO TO INSPIRE BEHAVIORAL SHIFTS IN THESE AREAS OF YOUR ANTIRACISM JOURNEY?

WRITE AN AFFIRMATION OF ENCOURAGEMENT FOR YOURSELF FAT THE END OF THIS ENTRY.

NOTES

CHANGE STARTED WITH ME

53686312R00148

Made in the USA
Columbia, SC
19 March 2019